C000148918

Podcasting

Beginner's Guide to Discovering Your Niche, Creating a Podcast
and Building and Growing a Profitable and Loyal Following

By Adam Torbert

circumstances is the author responsible for any losses, direct or indirect, which are incurred as a result of the use of information contained within this document, including, but not limited to, —errors, omissions, or inaccuracies.

Contents

Thank you for buying this book and I hope that you will find it useful. If you will want to share your thoughts on this book, you can do so by leaving a review on the Amazon page, it helps me out a lot.

Introduction

There has actually never ever been a greater time to begin your own podcast. Sales of mobile phones over previous years have actually created interest in podcasts and now there are more podcast listeners than ever prior.

A multitude of online marketers have actually attempted to produce a prosperous podcast and fell short. This due to the fact that they attempted to utilize out-of-date approaches to get their podcasts discovered, or since they simply didn't understand what they were doing. Now you can learn how to produce the greatest podcasts and develop a considerable following.

In this book you will be directed bit by bit through the procedure of producing a prosperous podcast. You are going to discover how to produce high-value and premium podcasts that listeners long for and how you can get the word out to your target market.

Preparing your podcasts is a really essential step in the procedure and lots of online marketers make the error of attempting to play it by ear. This is not the appropriate method and you are going to discover how to devote a small amount of time in preparation to produce the finest podcasts for your target market.

There are numerous manners in which you can monetize your podcasts and make substantial earnings from them monthly. Besides, it is going to require effort and time to create your podcasts so why not be compensated for it?

Utilize the methods in this book to produce truly prosperous podcasts. Offer your listeners the material that they desire and they are going to be starving for more. It is a lot simpler to stick out from the crowd with podcasting instead of video marketing and blogging if you have the appropriate methods to utilize.

Chapter 1: Potential of Podcasting

A great deal of online marketers dismiss podcasting since they do not think that it has the effect of videos- for instance. However, they are wrong to assume this due to the fact that a great deal of individuals like to listen to podcasts.

There are numerous prosperous podcasters out there that have a big following. Individuals enjoy their podcasts a great deal and they can't wait for the following one. You could be a sought-after podcaster and you can earn a profit from it too- which is what this book is everything about.

What is a Podcast?

A podcast is an audio production that is normally a series of episodes. It remains in MP3 format- which implies that you can get it and play it on any gadget that is going to play MP3 audio like:

- An MP3 player

- A tablet

- A smartphone

- A laptop computer

You may listen to a podcast while you are driving, however, you can not view a video. Podcast is like talk radio, however, it is on-demand instead of it being a constant program. There are podcasts offered on all sorts of topics and in a variety of various niches.

Are Podcasts Always Audios?

No not all the time. There are video podcasts that you can view on sites such as YouTube. They tend to present the podcast live with all of individuals included talking into mics. There are likewise videos on YouTube and other video sharing websites that are simply audios and they are going to have a fixed image (or often a variety of images).

Even if a podcast remains in video format, you can utilize a converter online to alter it to MP3 which is the sound component of the video. Then you can listen to the MP3 en route to work, in the gym, in the grocery store or anywhere you are.

A podcast actually resembles listening to a program on the radio. They are going to usually have a particular style, for instance, earning money online or pet training. The majority of the time, a podcast is going to be part of a series where it speaks about various elements of the subject.

A great deal of podcasts include more than a single person. The interview podcast is incredibly popular. Here the speaker is going to speak with a specialist on a specific topic. This is fantastic for the listener as they have the chance to gain from somebody that actually understands their things.

You are going to discover some podcasts that have sound effects and outro and intro tunes. This is easy to do. I would constantly urge you to create your podcasts as expertly as possible to ensure that your target market takes you seriously.

Why Should You Podcast?

The development in the variety of MP3-enabled phones has actually truly sustained interest in podcasts. Individuals now have a really simple and handy method to listen. There are a variety of other advantages to podcasting for the entrepreneur and the marketer:

A Nice Alternative to Video

A lot of online marketers would concur that video marketing is necessary nowadays. The issue with videos is that they take a great deal of time and preparation to film. Likewise, not everybody is cozy about showing up in videos. If you develop bad videos and it is apparent that you do not wish to show up in them, then this is going to do your enterprise more damage than good.

There are numerous videos out there nowadays, so it is a genuine challenge to make yours stick out from the crowd. You might have to buy truly costly software and tools to attain this. Numerous things can misfire when you film videos like the lighting, background noise and so on.

Podcasts are a lot less complicated to develop and the space is less packed so you can stick out far more quickly. All you require to produce a great podcast are a great audio editing software program suite and a top-quality microphone.

Use Podcast to Generate Traffic

When you develop and release podcasts, you are going to have the ability to connect to brand-new target markets. You can utilize podcasts to develop trust and likeability with a vast array of target markets. When a listener signs up for a podcast series, they are highly likely to tune in to every episode.

In the event that the listeners enjoy your podcast, then they are most likely to suggest it to other individuals who share the identical interests. When this word of mouth chips in, you can truly prolong your reach. You can create a great deal of targeted traffic to your site via podcasts.

You Can Form a Relationship with an Audience

It is feasible to develop a terrific connection with your audience via podcasting. The listeners are going to get the sensation that they truly know you after tuning in to a few of your podcasts.

All of this is a fantastic method for trust. Your listeners are going to create a solid association with your brand name and this is going to certainly assist you to offer more of your services or products. Your listeners are going to consider you as a buddy and they are going to be a lot more pleased to buy from a buddy than from an unfamiliar person.

You Can Easily Create Podcasts

There are not a great deal of actions associated with developing a high-quality podcast. Nowadays, you can acquire a lot of tools that you require at a really affordable cost. You have to buy a high-quality microphone for certain, and some high-quality earphones are going to likewise assist.

You are going to likewise require an audio editing suite, which you can download free of charge. This is going to allow you to do away with any mistakes and likewise include any jingles, outro and intro music and so forth. After you have actually finished your edits, you can produce your podcast in MP3 format extremely quickly to ensure that you can circulate it.

High Engagement

The Web is an excellent resource for any subject, however, there is often simply excessive information. It is a lot simpler to get a message across with a podcast as opposed to text. There was a study performed with 300,000 listeners and this exposed that 63% had actually acquired what the podcaster had suggested. This supports the reality that podcasts actually do engage an audience and can have a powerful impact on their purchasing conclusions.

Chapter 2: How to Choose a Niche

Among the greatest errors that individuals make with podcasting is that they do not pick the appropriate niche market. Due to the fact that it is fairly easy to develop a podcast, there is a temptation simply to leap right in without considering the future opportunities of what you are doing.

However, if you are serious about earning money through podcasting, then you have to select a specific niche that you are comfy with that is going to likewise offer you with profitable possibilities.

A great deal of "professionals" are going to inform you that you ought to pick a specific niche that you are enthusiastic about. This is especially essential with podcasting as the listeners are going to hear the enthusiasm in your voice.

However, the issue here is that not all "interests" pay. While there are lots of possible lucrative possibilities with a specific niche, such as dog training, there are a great deal less with model railways and stamp collecting.

So when you are thinking about a specific niche for your podcasts, you have to consider 2 essential elements: Is there a business opportunity and is there a demand?

You may be assuming at this phase that if you understand nothing about a specific niche that is in need and has great business possibilities, how could you be zealous about it? The response is that you can definitely end up being truly curious about a specific niche such as this, and when this occurs, your enthusiasm is going to appear.

Experts Have a Lot of Trust

When you pick a specific niche that is in need, you are going to obtain a lot more fans with your podcasts. Individuals who have an interest in the specific niche are going to instantly consider you as an authority even if you are not. Now I am not suggesting that you attempt to produce podcasts when you understand nothing about a specific niche-- that's simply stupid!

However, nowadays, you can discover a lot about a specific niche in a really brief time. There are a lot of resources on the internet and you can acquire top quality training courses for a great deal of various specific niches. You are going to have to put in some effort at first to get up to speed and you are going to wish to reach the point where you understand more about your specific niche than most individuals curious about it are going to understand.

This does not need to take you a number of years. Simply immerse yourself into the specific niche for a couple of days and you are going to find out a good deal. Here you are "faking it till you make it" which you may not feel that comfy with, however, after diving into your selected niche for some time, you are going to feel a great deal better about it all.

The very best method to develop yourself as a professional with your listeners is to supply them with beneficial pointers and guidance in your podcasts. Even if you are not popular, it is not going to take much time for the majority of your listeners to see you as an authority. When you have actually attained this, then you can begin suggesting relevant services and products.

So pick a sought-after niche with excellent business possibilities and persevere. Whatever you do, do not go dancing around from one specific niche to another. You are going to lose your listeners extremely rapidly in case you do this.

Choosing the Niche

The very best method to begin to determine your niche for podcasting is to jot down a list of your passions and interests. Likewise, write down specific niches that you understand a great deal about even if you do not think that you are enthusiastic about them.

Take a look at various podcasting sites to see which specific niches are the most prominent. Likewise, you can utilize the Keyword Planner from Google and see the number of searches taking place every month for niche ideas. In case there are thousands, then you may be on the appropriate path.

For every one of your niche ideas, utilize Google to discover if there are services and products offered, so you can end up being an affiliate for them and generate income. Simply look for "name of the niche" + affiliate programs.

You can likewise go to Clickbank.com and find if there are any digital items available there for your niche ideas. Clickbank is the global leader in digital items and they offer items in lots of various niches. You can likewise have a look at physical item possibilities on Amazon.com where you can end up being an affiliate and generate income.

Get rid of any niches that do not have the demand or adequate business possibilities, such as affiliate offers that you can market. As soon as you have actually accomplished that, you can proceed to the following action.

What Can You Do to Help People?

With the remaining niche ideas, jot down how you can assist individuals in every one. In each niche there are issues and at this phase simply recognize these and do not stress if you can fix them for individuals.

So, for instance, if one of your ideas was generating income online, then there are lots of issues here consisting of:

- Which is the most effective online business idea?

- How do I remain motivated?

- What is the most effective autoresponder?

These are the typee of questions that individuals thinking about the niche ask daily. You can discover the responses later on online. Having a variety of issues to resolve and the capability to supply answers for them is a powerful sign of a great niche.

Who are Your Competitors?

For the niche ideas that stay on your list, take a look at the competitors. Having competitors in a niche is a beneficial thing as it has a tendency to demonstrate that there is a need and, likewise, business possibilities.

Have a look at what type of podcasts your competitors are producing and think of how you can discover another angle or do it much better. Your goal is to stick out from the crowd. How much fans do your rivals have? What topics are they developing podcasts about?

If you truly love a niche idea, however, are worried that it does not have the appropriate level of business possibilities, then do not feel uneasy since there are a variety of manners in which you can generate income from the podcasts, which we are going to cover.

Chapter 3: Planning

So, you have actually selected your niche and you have actually determined a variety of issues that individuals in the niche have and understand how to address them. Is it time to begin capturing your podcasts? Well, almost...

You have to prepare your podcasts initially. How are you going to brand yourself? This is more than simply picking a fantastic name for your podcast or obtaining terrific cover art. It has to do with how you want your listeners to see your podcast. You have to get this right.

Mission and Vision

Prior to beginning, you have to develop a vision and mission for your podcasts. When you have actually accomplished this, then make sure to develop the best sort of material. To be sure we are on the identical page here, let's specify what vision and mission are.

Your mission is your objective for your podcast and how you mean to accomplish this. A vision is how you wish your podcasts to appear in the future. Both of these are actually crucial. As soon as you have actually specified your vision and mission, you can make sure that every released podcast lines up with them both.

Voice and Personality

Your podcasts will be a reflection of you. They are going to be special due to the fact that you are distinct. So, how can you make certain that you stay clear of that?

The ideal thing to do is to act normally when capturing your podcasts. There are no censors and no one is there evaluating you. You might wish to stay clear of utilizing particular words if you believe that they won't resonate properly with your audience.

You ought to constantly develop a memorable tagline for your podcast. Include something about your specific niche in your tagline and make it special and motivating. Take your time as you desire a tagline that will encourage brand-new listeners to check out your podcasts.

Consistency

Your individual branding is not simply restricted to your podcasts. It is ideal to be consistent with all platforms that you utilize. Utilize the identical branding on your site or blog site, your YouTube channel, Facebook page and anything else you utilize.

Get some excellent cover art produced for your brand name. In case you do not have any graphic design abilities, then go to Fiverr.com and pay a couple of dollars to somebody excellent to accomplish this for you. Utilize this cover art on every one of your platforms to ensure that your audience will quickly acknowledge it regardless of which one they are on.

If you do not do this, then you will frustrate individuals. With different branding for your social media channels and your podcast, for instance, your audience is not going to be certain that they are on the appropriate website.

Creating a Community

Individuals like communities as it supplies them with a feeling of belonging. The very best podcasters constantly cultivate a feeling of community with their listeners. You wish to do anything that you can to make all of your listeners feel extremely good. You want them to feel terrific.

You have to invest a bit of time into planning. This is time well invested as your listening audience is going to value what you are attempting to do for them. A strong community is going to constantly be on your side and they are going to want your excellent podcasts for a number of years.

Chapter 4: Necessary Tools

Prior to producing any podcasts, you require the appropriate tools. The worst thing that you may do is to create podcasts where the sound quality is bad. No one is going to wish to listen to them. A podcast is everything about audio and attempting to record utilizing the mic in your laptop computer or the one connected to a set of inexpensive earphones is not an option.

You have to consider the kind of podcasting you prepare to do. If you will have a configuration where visitors are going to show up on your podcasts by dropping into your house studio, then you are going to require a mixer and some other equipment. I do not recommend that you begin by doing this. It may cost you a great deal of cash to develop a small studio such as this.

I advise that you begin by developing the podcasts yourself and carrying out interviews over an app such as Skype. The benefit of doing this is that you can speak with individuals throughout the world. The drawback is that, in some cases, the quality of Skype recordings differ and the individual being spoken with are going to require an excellent microphone.

So we are going to have a look within this chapter at a house setup where you are going to utilize a pc for the recordings, and after that, we are going to go over the choices for establishing a small studio where visitors can come and make a podcast with you.

The Basic Recording Setup

This is the most basic kind of podcast recording arrangement that you may do in your home. You are going to require a computer system (which you most likely currently have), a top-quality microphone with a pop guard, audio editing software and high-quality earphones.

Most Computers Will Do

You do not require a high-end computer system to capture high-quality podcasts. Audio files are a lot tinier than video files and in case you have a fairly contemporary laptop or desktop, this ought to be more than adequate.

Mobile Devices for Recording

What about mobile phones? Well, you can capture a podcast on your tablet or mobile phone- however, you are going to require a better microphone than the one incorporated in your gadget. There are a variety of recording applications offered for sound for both iOS and Android gadgets. So mobile phone recording is definitely a possibility.

Microphone

In case you are simply going to utilize your computer system for solo podcasts and Skype interviews, then I suggest that you get a high-quality USB microphone. A USB microphone is going to work extremely well with your computer system. There are 2 various kinds of microphones, which are condenser and dynamic.

A condenser microphone is everything you require for solo recordings. If you mean to have 2 individuals on a podcast recording into your computer system, then dynamic microphones are ideal. You can discover high-quality USB microphones offered on Amazon for an affordable price. A number of fine examples are:

- The Blue Yeti, which is a condenser mic

- The Audio Technica ATR2100, a dynamic USB/XLR mic

In case you wish to capture utilizing your tablet or mobile phone, then you are going to require a much better microphone. You can utilize a lavalier microphone here, like the Rode smartLav+, which is an omnidirectional microphone which you can affix to a lapel for great recordings.

The Rode smartLav+ plugs directly into your tablet or mobile jack. This is a great choice if you intend to travel around to create podcast recordings. It is going to function on many iOS and Android mobile phones.

Have a Pop Guard

Some microphones feature a pop guard. In case your microphone does not come with this, then I highly suggest that you acquire one as it is going to enhance the sound quality of your podcasts considerably.

Mic Stand

You are going to require some kind of mic stand, otherwise you are going to need to hold your microphone when you are taping your podcasts. You may obtain a little desk stand for your microphone to ensure that it sits vertically on your desk. This suffices in many house recording circumstances.

Another method to hold a microphone in position is to utilize a boom arm. These are readily available independently or you can acquire them in a package with the mic-- the Blue Yeti microphone definitely has this possibility. You secure the boom arm to a desk, and after that, you can carry it around to ensure that it remains in the ideal setting for your recordings.

Headphones

Even though you can record a solo podcast on your computer system without earphones, I advise that you utilize a set of high-quality headphones for all of your recording, to ensure that you obtain live feedback on the quality.

You can pick in between "earbud" or "in-ear" earphones or the standard "over the ear" headphones. Among the ideal earbuds is the Panasonic Ergo Fit.

If you choose the over the ear earphones- then the AKG Pro Audio AKB K92 closed-back earphones offer terrific sound at an excellent cost. Obviously, there are better over the ear earphones offered and if you desire the most ideal, then the Grado SR352e is the right choice.

Audio Editing

When you capture your podcasts, it is extremely improbable that you are not going to wish to make some edits. You might have made some errors that you wish to cut for the last production, and you can make your podcasts sound expert by including sound effects and outro and intro music.

Here are some great news. After investing cash in a great microphone and other add-ons, there is no requirement for you to spend for audio editing software. There are 2 cost-free audio editing sets which are going to offer all of the resources that you require to create top quality podcasts:

- Windows computer systems-- Audacity

- Mac computer systems—Garageband

There are other audio editing sets and a few of which are free of charge. In all sincerity,

Garageband and Audacity are all you require, so why spend for an editing set when you do not have to?

I won't describe how to utilize these audio editing sets here as it is outside the range of this book. There are lots of videos on YouTube that are going to demonstrate how to utilize the standard and sophisticated functions of these audio tools.

If you wish to do your audio editing on your tablet or mobile phone, then there are a variety of paid and free apps offered for this. For Android gadgets, there is WaveEditor, for instance, and for iOS, you can utilize TonePad or Garageband.

It is not the simplest thing to edit your recordings on a mobile phone with these apps. So a more desirable choice would be to save your preliminary recording in MP3 format on your phone utilizing an app, and after that, transfer it onto your computer system and utilize Garageband or Audacity.

The Advanced Setup

If you wish to produce a podcast recording studio, then you are going to require some extra tools. You are going to have to utilize vibrant microphones with an XLR connecter for plugging into a mixer. You are going to likewise require the mixer, perhaps a preamp, a digital recorder and a variety of boom arms to keep the mics in position.

The concept here is that you are going to develop your podcasts utilizing a digital recorder and the mixer, and after that, move the recording onto your computer system to ensure that you can carry out your edits with Garageband or Audacity.

To develop a podcasting studio such as this will take some major financial investment, so you have to make sure that this is what you want. This is a perfect setup if you remain in a great area where visitors can quickly drop in and take part in podcasts with you.

Chapter 5: Planning for Greatness

Prior to recording your initial podcast, you have a prepare for it. Podcasts captured "on the fly" hardly ever end up that well. You have to get ready for every podcast to guarantee that things go as efficiently as feasible.

You do not have to invest hours in a podcast strategy. Investing a bit of time into a strategy is going to make a big distinction to the quality of every one of your podcasts.

Organizing your Podcasts

You won't make simply one podcast, so it is an excellent strategy to get arranged to ensure that you can record and prepare your podcasts regularly. There are no stringent guidelines for the number of podcasts you ought to produce a month, however, constantly bear in mind that it is not a great strategy to keep your listeners standing by for too long as they are going to discover another individual's podcast!

I advise that you have a calendar for your podcasting tasks. You have the choice of pen and paper or technology. If you choose technology, then I suggest that you utilize Google Calendar. There are paid choices, however, the cost-free Google Calendar is going to do every little thing that you require.

With Google Calendar, you can include a description to the items that you create. So you can include the subject of every podcast for the following couple of weeks for instance. You can even connect files to your calendar if you wish to. Simply do anything you have to do to be arranged with your podcast recording and preparation.

What to Talk About

You have to devote the most time to planning what you will speak about on your podcast. If you mess this up, then it matters not just how much expensive devices you have; your podcast is going to be a catastrophe.

Constantly remember that your podcasts are for your listeners. So you have to supply recordings that your target market is going to actually appreciate. Do your research here and learn what your audience desires. You may ask yourself these questions to assist you:

- What concerns do your listeners have?

- What issues do your listeners have?

- What things are your listeners dealing with now?

Utilize a response to one of these in your podcasts. One manner in which you can quickly learn what your audience is trying to find is to perform some keyword research. Utilizing the cost-free Keyword Planner from Google, you can find the search terms that individuals in your specific niche are utilizing to discover responses to their concerns and issues.

Keyword research is an actually excellent strategy due to the fact that you can produce a list of pertinent keywords for your specific niche that you utilize for podcast episodes and for enhancing your listings when you disperse your recordings. We are going to speak about this more later on in this book.

Another manner in which you can develop material for your podcasts is by brainstorming. If you make a podcast with other individuals, then ask for their suggestions too. You are going to get a much better outcome if you utilize their suggestions along with your ideas.

Utilize a mind map if you will film solo. This is going to assist you to think through all of the relationships with your preliminary podcast concept and can even assist you with thinking of motifs for future podcasts.

Have a Script

A few of you may not like the concept of developing a script for your podcast, however, it truly is going to assist you. If you are a professional in your specific niche, then you might not require a complete script to follow. Simply jot down the crucial points that you wish to cover, and after that, utilize these as triggers. You are going to have to be quite positive to create a great podcast utilizing triggers.

When you compose an in-depth script, it offers you with an actually tight method to produce a podcast that is loaded with good stuff. Having a complete script is going to stop you from babbling on and is going to likewise guarantee that you cover all the things in your podcast.

There are a number of issues with a comprehensive script, however. First is the quantity of effort and time that it is going to require you to compose it. Second is that an in-depth script can stop you from being casual and stop you from including your character.

I suggest that you develop a number of test podcasts by utilizing a "timely" script and a comprehensive script and see which one fits you better. Listen seriously to test recordings and look for coverage of points. Ultimately, practice is the way. Eventually, you are going to discover the ideal type of script for you to produce the ideal podcasts.

It is much better if you have some kind of script than no script. Even if you have a fantastic memory, the tension of creating the podcast recording can lead you to forget specific points that you truly wished to cover. Start by utilizing an in-depth script, and after that, see if you can manage with a timely script as you get more experience.

Recording Interviews

Your listeners are going to typically eagerly anticipate interviews with specialists in your specific niche. In case your expert lives far, then the ideal option is to capture your discussion utilizing an online application. There are a couple of excellent apps available that you can utilize for this:

Skype

Skype is an exceptionally popular online call app that has actually improved considerably throughout the years. A great deal of individuals have Skype accounts, so talk to your interviewee beforehand to ensure that they can rapidly establish a Skype account for free in case they do not have one.

There are a variety of apps offered for capturing Skype calls and developing MP3 files. There is, in fact, a function now in Skype to capture calls. As soon as you have actually begun your call, you can begin recording and both sides are alerted that the recording has actually started. You can pause the recording at any moment or it is going to instantly stop by the end of the call.

When the recording has actually wrapped up, Skype produces an MP4 file and includes it in the chat window where you may download it. You are going to then need to change this into an MP3 file for editing. At the moment, all audios are in mono format. This is not excellent for stabilizing recording levels in your editor.

The following level for Skype call recording is either Call Recorder for Mac computer systems or TalkHelper for windows computer systems. You are going to need to pay a tiny premium for these apps. They are going to capture both sides in different channels to ensure that you can balance the volume. You likewise obtain the audio file.

Zoom

Zoom is more advanced, as it is more akin to a video conferencing tool. All you have to do is utilize Zoom to establish an area and send out the created link to the other individual to ensure that they can sign in.

All calls utilizing Zoom are immediately captured, and you are going to get an audio file when the call has actually concluded. You can establish the recording to ensure that it is going to capture the two sides on various channels, which is terrific for editing. If you are just taping with one individual, then a Zoom call is cost-free.

Whenever you will capture an interview utilizing Skype, Zoom or any other approach, you ought to prepare the questions that you can ask and verify this with the interviewee before the interview.

Chapter 6: Creating Professional Podcasts

Listeners of your podcast will evaluate it on 2 things: The quality of the audio and the quality of the material you offer.

I will presume that you followed the recommendations on preparing your podcast and are going to produce important material for your audience. Now, we are going to take a look at how you can produce podcasts like a pro.

Proper Recording

If you tape your podcast properly, then this is going to spare you from investing a great deal of time into editing it. There is very little fun in dealing with a great deal of errors. If there are numerous mistakes in your recording, it may even be faster for you to capture the entire thing once more.

it is not likely that you will produce recordings with no errors in them, specifically when you are simply beginning. However, you can do a fair bit to decrease the amount of errors in a podcast recording by adhering to these rules:

Record in a Quiet Place

You would assume that this would be apparent, however, a great deal of individuals make the error of capturing their podcasts in a loud environment. Then they need to devote a lot of time attempting to edit out disruptive background noises (often, this is not even feasible).

Select a peaceful place for your recording and make certain to close doors and windows. Switch off your phone, or at minimum, place it in silent mode. Inform other individuals in your house that you will be capturing a podcast, and not to disrupt you unless there is a crisis.

Speak Clearly

I stated prior that you should use earphones when you are capturing your podcasts. If you do not utilize any earphones, then you will not understand precisely how you are sounding. You might be speaking too softly or loudly.

Utilize earphones and speak straight into your microphone. If you read a script, then make certain that you do this without turning your head far from the mic. Listen in your earphones and see if you have to make some changes to your recording software, like the volume, the tone, the cadence, and so forth.

Each Person Has to Have a Microphone

If there are 2 or more individuals associated with your podcast, then offer each of them with their own mic. You might believe that you can share a microphone, however, the outcome won't be terrific and you are going to devote a great deal of time towards editing.

Putting a single microphone between 2 individuals taking part in a podcast seldom turns out well. Individuals speak at various volumes and one can quickly muffle the other.

Have a Test Recording

It is often a great idea to carry out some testing initially prior to you trying to capture your podcast. There are a variety of things that can misfire, like you not connecting the mic correctly or you having it on mute!

Can you picture capturing a 60-minute podcast just to find that you had not captured anything? These things occur, so do a test initially. With your test, you can see that your recording levels are correct, there is no background sound, you have your recording software set up properly, and so on

Editing

You need to intend to supply your listeners with the greatest experience with each podcast that you release. It is very probable that your listeners are going to be doing another thing when they are tuning in to your podcast. This indicates that you have to decrease any diversions. Your listeners will be frustrated if they hear your heavy breathing, loud noises or any other thing that will sidetrack them from what you are offering in your podcast. If you do not look after these things, then you are going to wind up with bad reviews. When you have actually captured your podcast, you have to listen to all of it.

You have to understand how to make edits, so learn this on YouTube or through tutorials on their site. Carry out the required edits as you go along. In case you sneeze or cough while you are speaking, then you absolutely wish to cut these out. Here is an excellent idea-- you are going to understand when you have actually slipped up throughout the recording. So straight after the error, leave a number of seconds of quiet to ensure that you can carry out smooth edits later on. After carrying out all of the required edits, tune in to the audio once again. It is feasible that you might have overlooked something. Place yourself in the shoes of a listener and truthfully evaluate whether you have actually developed a terrific listening experience.

Creating a Podcast File

When you are delighted with all of the editing and the podcast sounds actually great, then it is time to include your outro and intro music and any additional effects. You can include these on various tracks in your audio editor. Make certain that you listen to the entire thing once again prior to producing your last file.

In many audio editors, you are going to then carry out a "mix down" where all of the various tracks are transformed into a single track. You may then save this in MP3 format to ensure that it is prepared for you to release to the globe.

49

Prior to submitting your file, include metadata or ID3 tags. Here you are going to supply the essential details so that your listeners can see crucial information about your podcast. This are going to be things such as the name of the podcast, the summary, the number, and so forth.

Including your ID3 tags in editing apps like Garageband and Audacity is actually simple and there are a variety of videos on YouTube that are going to demonstrate to you precisely how to accomplish this.

Chapter 7: Hosting and Distribution

You are going to have to host your podcast files to ensure that your listeners can access them. They are going to either stream your podcast or download it. In case you have web hosting with unrestricted disk area, then you might believe that you can simply submit your files. However, you can encounter problems if you carry this out.

Endless disk area is generally for web files. MP3 or audio files are not classified as web files. So the ideal thing to do is to utilize a podcast hosting service. These services are made for the serving and storage of sound files of various sizes.

Among the advantages of utilizing a podcast hosting service is that they have actually confirmed and embedded RSS feeds. These RSS feeds are certified with the podcasting directory sites that make the submission procedure simple for you and connectivity to your podcasts simple for your listeners.

You can utilize your RSS feed link when you create submissions to the podcast directory sites. Every time you publish a brand-new podcast file to your host, then the directories where you have actually sent your RSS feed are going to all immediately get the update. Your listeners are going to likewise instantly get your brand-new podcasts on the gadget of their selection.

Another excellent reason for utilizing a podcast hosting company is that you are going to have the ability to gain access to stats regarding your podcasts. Depending upon the podcast company that you utilize, you are going to have the ability to see some helpful information about your listeners like:

- Download numbers

- Apps utilized to tune in to the podcast

- Sources of traffic

- Listener areas

You are going to likewise have the ability to develop a podcast page with your podcasting host. Here you can offer info about your podcasts and incorporate banners, podcast notes, your social networks, and more. You can connect to your blog site or site from this page as well.

This podcast page is going to likewise consist of a media player where individuals can stream your podcasts utilizing their internet browser. They are going to likewise have the ability to download your podcasts, sign up for them, and share them from this page.

While there are cost-free accounts offered with a variety of podcast hosts, I would constantly advise that you opt for the paid alternative as the expenses are normally low. 2 prominent podcast hosting options are LibSyn and PodBean which have options beginning with $3 a month.

Podcast Distribution

I suggest that you capture a couple of podcasts initially prior to dispersing them. It appears a lot better if you have a couple of various podcasts offered instead of simply one. As soon as you have actually done this, you are prepared to get the word out and inform the world about your remarkable podcasts.

Directories

You are going to wish to send your podcasts to a variety of podcasting directory sites. The main ones will have the most traffic (iTunes obtains the most without a doubt), so I recommend that you send your podcasts to these:

- iTunes

- Spotify

- Google Play

- TuneIn

- Stitcher

- SoundCloud

There is no reason why you should not search for additional podcasting directories. The more of them that you utilize, the more individuals you can reach. Bear in mind that when you utilize a podcast RSS feed link, you are going to just need to produce a single submission.

What about YouTube? You definitely need to have your podcasts on YouTube. You are going to need to transform the MP3 to MP4 format, however, this is simple to do with a cost-free online converter. YouTube is going to decline a podcast RSS feed, so you are going to have to submit one at a time. Make sure to optimize correctly so your podcasts are going to be discovered.

Use your Private Network

Do not simply leave it to podcast directory submissions to spread the word about your podcasts. Have a look at your private network, consisting of your members of the family, buddies, associates and acquaintances.

Do not be timid about your podcasts! You have actually put a great deal of effort into developing truly worthwhile podcasts so ask your private network to assist you in marketing them. Even if they are not curious about your podcast niche, they are going to know individuals that you do not that might be curious.

Ask individuals that you know to listen to the podcasts, and after that, leave a favorable review for you on iTunes or the various directories. Reviews are vital for your growth, so do all the things that you may to obtain them. When others find your reviews, they are going to be a lot more probable to tune in to your podcasts.

Online Promotion

In case you have your own blog or site, then advertise your podcasts there. In case you have an e-mail list, then send a broadcast e-mail to everybody letting them know where they can discover your podcats and asking for a review.

Compose a post particularly about your brand-new podcasts and release this on your website. You can include banners to your website, promoting your podcasts. When you publish your podcasts to YouTube, you can embed these into your blog site as particular posts.

In case you have existing social networks, then make certain to create posts about your podcasts there. You can utilize your private Facebook account to create a post, and after that, direct individuals to your Facebook page to learn more, for instance.

Use Influencers

Nowadays, it is an excellent suggestion to utilize influencer marketing. The concept here is that you are going to take advantage of brand names or people that have big followings on their social networks, podcasts, blog sites, and so forth.

Whenever these individuals recommend something, their fans are going to generally go and check it out. So attempt and discover influencers where you can collaborate for shared advantage. Do your research here to discover influencers that actually do have a strong level of engagement and not a load of phony fans. Contact them and work out an offer.

Interview Experts

We discussed this in previous chapters. Individuals enjoy being viewed as specialists in their niche, so discover individuals that you think can bring value to your podcasts and connect with them and ask for an interview.

It is ideal to interview specialists that have a big following at first. You wish for these specialists to market your program to their fan base. When you have actually developed a great following of your own, you can speak with specialists that do not have a big following as well.

When a specialist accepts be interviewed for a podcast, make certain that you send them a link to ensure that they can access the last recording. You can develop a personalized swipe file to assist your specialist to promote your podcasts for you, consisting of social network posts, emails and other manners in which they can inform their following.

Constantly thank any professionals that you speak with for their time and providing their insight with your listeners. Likewise, thank them for sharing the podcast with their fanbase. If they wish to interview you, then constantly accept this. This is a fantastic chance for you to establish yourself as a professional as well, and advertise your podcasts too, naturally.

Paid Ads

There is no reason why you should not utilize paid advertisements to get the word out. I would advise that you utilize Facebook Ads to accomplish this as you can determine your target market exactly. It is still quite affordable to utilize Facebook Ads to get to your target market.

Obviously, Facebook isn't the only option and there are additional platforms that are going to gladly take your cash for advertising your podcasts. Do your research and set yourself a spending plan to ensure that you do not spend beyond your means on marketing.

You are going to get the most out of paid marketing when you truly understand your target market!

Chapter 8: Promotions and Offers

There is definitely no reason why you should not advertise associated deals in your podcasts. They are your podcasts, so you may do what you desire. No one will attempt and persecute you for advertising in your own podcasts.

It is a great deal simpler to stand apart with podcasting than with other kinds of media. The opposition in podcasting is a lot lesser than video, and in case you have had the nerve to capture your voice and publish it, then you ought to receive something in return for your work. Simply follow these actions to advertise deals in an ideal manner:

Be Subtle

I would strongly advise that you get a couple of podcasts under your belt and develop a following prior to offering deals. When you do begin with the promotion of deals, do not make it too sales-focused as your listeners are not going to be delighted with this.

Initially, it is going to take a while for your listeners to be familiar with you, so do not strike them with deals right from the start. This is extremely improbable to work and you are going to most likely lose a great deal of listeners if you do so. You have to be more refined.

I know that you have actually put in a good deal of effort and time (and most likely cash) to produce your podcasts. You wish to get a return immediately. However, you need to have patience with podcasting and your advertising messages need to be subtle.

Among the ideal methods for making a promo is to point out it in the outro and intro of your podcast. So at the start of the podcast, inform the listeners of who you are and offer a bit of background. Then reveal your deal and inform your listeners that there are more details in the podcast notes if they are curious. Begin the podcast generally after this.

When your podcast concludes, simply carefully remind your listeners about your deal and let them know to take a look at the notes and description for more information. You are sharing the details with your market-- there is no hard selling included.

Offering Value

All of your podcasts have to have value and you have to consider an excellent way to interleave your deal into this. An excellent way to do this is to talk about pain points with your listeners and letting them know that you have the response to their issues and can alleviate their problem. The response, obviously, is your deal.

Inform your listeners about the advantages they are going to get by checking out your offer today. Describe that the item is going to offer the answers to their issues. Assist them by directing them on how to utilize the item to ensure that they can benefit.

This technique is a valuable one instead of a sales-focused one. You are teaching your listeners how they can fix a few of their issues, which is going to be valued. Naturally, they are going to have to buy your deal to learn precisely what they have to do, however, that is okay.

Individuals do not want to be sold to, however, they are going to constantly value it if you are attempting to assist them. This is the promo technique that you have to utilize with your podcasts. Other effective podcasters have actually been carrying this out for a number of years due to the fact that it works so effectively.

Provide Alternative Offers

The identical deal is most likely not going to fit effectively with all of your podcasts, so you have to have some alternate deals lined up that are going to assist your listeners. Never ever be timid when it pertains to promoting another deal-- if you do not have an item of your own that is an excellent fit, you can promote somebody else's item for a commission.

Your goal with any deals that you make is helping your listeners. If an affiliate item is the ideal method to do that, then opt for this. Your listeners are going to appreciate you for allowing them to understand that these items exist to assist with resolving their issues.

Constantly advertise quality services and products. If you will advertise an affiliate deal, then take a look yourself initially. If you advertise something of bad quality, then your track record is going to take a fall and you might reverse all of the effort.

Chapter 9: How to Grow Your Podcast

You have to do every little thing you can to expand your podcast listener numbers. We are going to go over a few of the most effective techniques to do this within this chapter. It won't be simple, however, with the correct amount of resolution, you can grow your podcast audience considerably.

It is vital that you are consistent. This indicates that you need to constantly offer something good to your listeners and that you release a brand-new podcast regularly. The frequency of publishing falls to you-- it could be weekly, fortnightly and even daily if you have the material and time to accomplish this.

As you grow your listener base, they are going to get accustomed to your podcast schedule. They are going to be really dissatisfied if you skip a week, for instance. So you have to get arranged for podcast production as we talked about in an earlier chapter and provide your listeners with what they desire when they want it.

Let's presume that you will release a brand-new podcast once a week. Select the identical day to release. So if you release a brand-new podcast every Friday, then your listeners are going to enter into the routine of tuning into your podcast channel each Friday and anticipate a brand-new podcast to be there.

Some listeners are going to organize their lives around your podcast. They are going to download your podcast and listen to it as they are doing another thing. So do not disappoint them! If you begin skipping Fridays, then they are going to quickly lose confidence in your channel and look in other places.

I highly advise that you capture a number of podcasts ahead of time to ensure that publishing weekly is a lot simpler for you. So, for instance, you might capture 3 podcasts over a weekend, which covers you for the next month.

Reviews are Crucial

You won't motivate brand-new listeners if you do not have any great scores or reviews. Even worse than this is to have a plethora of bad reviews on your channel. Individuals have actually ended up being familiar with searching for reviews prior to acting. They do not wish to be the initial one to attempt something even when it is cost-free.

You need to supply adequate proof to a brand-new listener that listening to your podcasts will be a great utilization of their time. Favorable scores and reviews are the very best method to do this. So ask your listeners to offer a score and review for your podcasts at every chance.

What takes place if you get an unfavorable review? Well, the initial thing to do is to observe if the review is warranted. If it is, then you have to learn from it and thank the individual for their remarks and say that you are going to take their ideas on board.

In some cases, bad reviews pertain to a smear campaign. If you believe this, then call the podcast directory administrator and request the comments to be deleted. Regrettably, some individuals are going to go to any lengths to attempt and undermine their rivals.

When you have a truly big listener base, there is constantly a likelihood that you are going to get some bad reviews. You have to be strong when this occurs and react quickly to the comments. You can't please everybody.

If your reviews are generally favorable, then no one will mind a couple of unfavorable reviews. Have a look at your podcast stats and if you find that your podcasts are being downloaded and streamed in substantial numbers, then tell yourself that you are on the correct path. Do not be discouraged by the minority.

Ask your loved ones to leave a couple of favorable reviews to get you began. You require something for prospective listeners to find.

Promoting your Podcasts

Many prosperous online marketers devote about 20% of their time to producing content and the other 80% on advertising. You have to do this also. Even if you created it, it does not imply that listeners are going to come. Constant advertising of your podcasts is the very best method.

The initial step is to actually understand who your target market is. When you understand this, you can learn where they hang out. If your audience is more youthful, then they are going to most likely utilize Instagram, Reddit, Snapchat, etc and if they are older then attempt Pinterest, Facebook, and online forums, for instance.

So in case your audience will on Facebook, you can utilize Facebook Ads to connect with them. Facebook has an excellent retargeting system which suggests that if an individual demonstrates a preliminary interest, they get "cookied", and after that, you can retarget them once more.

A retargeted person is warm. They have actually currently found you and your brand name and it is a lot easier to turn them than it is with leads that are cold. You can utilize a reward to transform both warm and cold leads and get them onto your e-mail list. Once they have actually signed up, let them know about your podcasts.

Contests

When you have a great quantity of listeners, you can hold a contest. Some instances might be:

- The best Facebook post about your podcasts

- The greatest tagline idea for your podcast program

Consider what you wish to attain here. Do you desire more individuals to leave a post on Facebook about your podcast to ensure that you can boost your reach? Or do you wish to acquire more great reviews on your channel?

Constantly offer the contest winner an excellent reward for getting involved. If you have actually produced your own items, then you might offer the winner access to this free of charge. You can get some top quality products (e.g. USB sticks) and offer these to the runners up, for instance.

Constantly call the winner on one of your podcasts and connect to them and ask if they wish to be talked to. Let them know that they may have a one-minute slot to advertise their enterprise if they wish to.

Chapter 10: Making Money With Podcasts

We have currently covered that you can offer deals throughout your podcasts to folks to acquire your services or products or an affiliate deal where you get a commission. However, it does not need to end there. There are a variety of other manners in which you can generate income from your podcasts.

Ask for Donations.

A great deal of effective podcasters utilize a donation service such as Patreon as a method to gather contributions from their listeners. You can introduce this on every one of your podcasts and inform your listeners that it is an excellent method for them to assist you to develop more podcasts down the road.

Discover Sponsorship and Partners

Among the most typical methods to generate income from a podcast is with sponsorship. This is fantastic for you as you do not need to do any selling. Generally, a sponsor is going to ask you to include a particular line at the start and perhaps the conclusion of your podcast.

Naturally, a broker is going to desire a cut of the sponsorship or advertisement cash, however, they are worth utilizing due to the fact that they are in contact with a great deal of businesses that are seeking to sponsor podcasts. It is a lot easier than searching for sponsors on your own.

Have Premium Content

When you have a developed listener base, you can produce premium podcasts that your listeners need to pay to gain access to. Some suggestions for premium podcasts are:

- Q & A sessions

- Interviews with renowned specialists.

Make Money from YouTube

You can make extra earnings by syndicating your podcasts on YouTube and registering for Google Adsense. When individuals are listening to your podcasts on YouTube, they are going to be provided with appropriate advertisements. Due to the fact that you are not utilizing video, these advertisements are going to appear a lot less invasive. You are going to get a commission for the advertisements that are clicked.

Offer Coaching or Consulting Services

Your listeners view you as a specialist and a complete authority in your specific niche. They would like to learn what you know. You can provide your listeners with a series of pricey training or consulting sessions.

Play Around With Various Monetization Approaches

Test to see which money-making techniques work ideally with your podcasts. There are other methods that you can utilize to make some cash. Sponsorship and contributions are the most typical kind of monetization. They generate routine earnings without you needing to do a lot.

Conclusion

You now have all the things that you require to prepare for and produce an effective and lucrative podcast. I highly suggest that you develop objectives for your podcast and that you deliver on value, and the audio quality for your podcasts.

Podcasting provides an incredible chance for individual marketers and businesses. If somebody informs you that podcasting does not work, then they merely do not understand what they are speaking about.

With a prosperous podcast, you have the chance to create leads and sales of affiliate deals and your items. Eventually, you can try to find sponsors who are going to pay you routine month-to-month earnings for a shout out.

It is essential that you are regular with your podcasts. Make a dedication to posting one time a week, for instance, and make certain that your brand-new podcasts appear on the identical day every week. Your listeners are going to enter into the routine of searching for your podcast every week with anticipation.

You have to take action and follow the recommendations in this book. Do not bypass any steps in the procedure. Devote the majority of your time marketing your podcast. Get going today with your podcasting. I wish you success with your podcasting and earning a profit from this really neglected type of marketing!

I hope that you enjoyed reading through this book and that you have found it useful. If you want to share your thoughts on this book, you can do so by leaving a review on the Amazon page. Have a great rest of the day.

Printed in Great Britain
by Amazon